SYSTEMS THINKING
FOR
CURIOUS MANAGERS

WITH **40** NEW MANAGEMENT f-LAWS

RUSSELL L. ACKOFF

WITH

HERBERT J. ADDISON AND ANDREW CAREY

FOREWORD BY JAMSHID GHARAJEDAGHI

tp

Published in this first edition in 2010 by:
Triarchy Press
Axminster
United Kingdom

+44 (0)1297 561335
info@triarchypress.net
www.triarchypress.net

A catalogue record for this book is available from the British Library.

Cover design by Heather Fallows ~
www.whitespacegallery.org.uk

ISBN: 978-0-9562631-5-5

Contents

Foreword

RUSSELL L. ACKOFF (1919-2009)

Jamshid Gharajedaghi, Managing Partner, Interact

Sadly, my great mentor, dear friend and business partner of the last thirty years, Russell L. Ackoff, died (29th October, 2009). This is a tribute to his wonderful memories and Herculean contributions to systems thinking. I am deeply honored by the invitation to write this foreword.

Talking about Russ Ackoff is not an easy proposition. His uniqueness and multidimensionality defies conventional wisdom. He was forceful and yet kind; caring but not compromising; fearsome but dependable. For me, he was the epitome of wholeness, bringing complementary opposites into a harmonious whole.

As a friend he was both unforgiving and empowering. He seemed merciless in making you confront your weaknesses, expecting and accepting nothing but the very best from his friends. While at the same time, he was equally tireless in promoting you as nothing but the very best.

As a mentor he was challenging – and a challenge – and yet as a colleague you could count on him to be always there, rock solid, when you needed him.

As a systems thinker, the sheer magnitude of his contributions places him in a class by himself. Russ was the founder of two distinct paradigms in systems thinking: Operations Research (OR) and Interactive Design. With Operations Research, he dealt with the challenge of interdependency in the context of 'mindless systems'. With Interactive Design, he faced the triple challenge of interdependency, self-organization and choice in the context of 'multi-minded systems'.

I got to know Ackoff during the sixties when I was an IBMer with the assignment to learn Operations Research to help clients who had become interested in its applications.

Foreword

Operations Research was the first attempt at creating an operational systems methodology. It uses mathematical modeling to find optimal solutions in the face of complex sets of interdependent variables. The initial version of OR was developed and used by the military during World War II. In the fifties, Russell Ackoff and West Churchman created the first academic OR program at the Case Institute of Technology. By the mid sixties, Case had become a mecca for Operations Researchers and the profession had advanced to such a level that most well known universities had incorporated an OR program in one form or another.

But my fascination with OR only lasted for a few years. After implementing a few projects with a group of clients, I learned that decision makers, despite their willingness to pay handsomely for the work, were not really interested in the optimum solution. They were only interested in confirming the choices they had already made.

Hoping to find an answer to the question of why people do what they do, I was drawn towards the living systems paradigm, or biological thinking, that was gradually replacing the machine mode of organization. Cybernetics (the second generation of systems methodology), despite its elegance and phenomenal success in dealing with the dynamic behavior of 'self-maintaining' and 'goal-seeking' systems, in my experience, was unable to deal with the complexities of 'purposeful' systems where parts displayed choice and behaved independently. This would be the equivalent of a thermostat developing a mind of its own!

When we met in 1974, Ackoff with his famous purposeful systems[1] had bypassed biological thinking and was ready to face the core problem of choice in the behavior of multi-minded social systems.

With this extraordinary leap he left his contemporaries twenty-five years behind. And at the same time, with sheer excellence and hard work, he defied the conventional wisdom that being ahead of your time is more tragic than falling behind.

But the dominant academic culture had no interest in disturbing its well-groomed analytical approach to include the messy notion of

---

1   Ackoff, R. L. and Emery, F. E. (1972). *On Purposeful Systems*. Chicago: Aldine-Atherton.

choice. Russ was forced to confront the old guard at every turn of his distinguished career.

That career can be viewed in three distinct phases. The fifties and sixties were all about OR. During the seventies he struggled to save OR from the wrong turn he believed it had taken. Finally, in 1979, he gave up on OR, claiming that 'the future of OR is past' and thus converting an army of dedicated followers into staunch enemies. The third phase – the last 30 years of his life – were all devoted to Interactive Design. He was the first to consider design as a systems methodology. As early as 1974, he told me that design is the vehicle through which choice is manifested, and design would be the future of systems methodology. Science is about what it is, design on the other hand is about what it ought to be. These words of his still ring in my ears: 'The future is not contained in the past, much of it is yet to be written and designers have a lot to say about it.'

Ironically, Interactive Design, 35 years after its inception, is still more potent and profound than what has recently emerged as 'design thinking'. Ackoff's formulation goes much further than being just a vehicle for the enhancement of innovation. It aims at the core of social transformation. The beauty of Interactive Design, for me, has been in its answer to the following postulation:

> Self-organizing purposeful socio-cultural systems are self-evolving. Guided by an implicit shared image, they tend to reproduce a familiar pattern of existence. To change this pattern, the shared image – itself a complex design – needs to be changed. This can only be done by the participation of relevant actors in the redesign process. Designers are to replace the existing order by operationalizing their most exciting vision of the future, the design of the next generation of the system. The desired future is then realized by successive approximation.

For Russ, choice is at the heart of human development, but choice without competence is meaningless. He exemplified a novel notion in political philosophy that considers colorlessness and the loss of individuality to be as threatening to social sanity as the tyranny of the majority.

~

Ackoff was, first and foremost, an educator. His Social Systems Sciences (known as S3) program at the Wharton School (from 1974 to 1986) was the largest Ph.D. program at Wharton with well over 100 students. Despite its unconventionality, it was the only Systems program that enjoyed the status of a formal Department in a major university. In S3, students and faculty learned together a topic that they had chosen together in 'Learning Cells' and went after new knowledge in 'Research and/or Design Cells.'

Born on February 12, 1919, he received a Bachelor of Architecture in 1941 and a Ph.D. in Philosophy of Science (1947) from the University of Pennsylvania. He served in the U.S. army during World War II, from 1942 to 1946. Before retiring from Wharton in 1986 he was Chairman of the Social Systems Science Department and Director of the Busch Center for Systems Research. In 1986, Ackoff and a group of colleagues from the Busch Center formed Interact – The Institute for Interactive Management. Interact became his professional home for the next twenty years until he retired in 2006.

Ackoff authored twenty-eight books, many of which have been translated into several languages. He also published more than 200 articles in books and journals. He was a charter member and former president of the Operations Research Society of America, founding member and former vice president of the Institute of Management Sciences, and former president of the Society for General Systems Research (now ISSS). He received six honorary degrees and a number of medals. He was elected a member of both the Academy of Natural Sciences for the Russian Federation and The International Academy of Management.

Russell Ackoff, as researcher, consultant, and educator, touched and influenced more than 350 corporations and 75 government agencies in the United States and around the globe.

~

Ackoff, above all his greatness, was a wonderful friend and exceptional human being; the world will be a much less likeable place without him and I will miss him very much. I trust the beautiful and provocative ideas presented in this book will continue to serve as a reminder of his greatness.

Jamshid Gharajedaghi
November 2009

Introduction

'The situation the world is in is a *mess.*' So said Russ Ackoff in a paper he gave in 2004.[1] Back then there were many who would have agreed with him and many more who wouldn't. Today, few would argue with his analysis. The world and its financial, economic, geopolitical and social systems – as well as its ecosystem, of course – feel increasingly fragile and unstable. And we are constantly reminded that everything is connected: the melting of a glacier in Greenland or the collapse of a bank in Berlin may have an extraordinary and devastating effect on the lives of people on the other side of the world.

Professor Ackoff was in the habit of drawing our attention to this *mess* all his life. Not because he was some modern-day Jeremiah, but because of his clear and simple insight that things could be so much better. Education, healthcare, town planning, local government, management, business, international relations – all of them, for Ackoff, fell lamentably far short of their potential. And all have found themselves in the limelight at one time or another as he turned his attention to them.

Remarkably for an academic, Russ Ackoff not only wrote at length chastising our political, social and business leaders for this falling short, but he also explained at great length how we could do better. As Jamshid Gharajedaghi describes in his foreword, Ackoff wrote, lectured and consulted at the most senior level on all these topics – offering a clear vision of what things could be like, and how to get there. (As a result he often appeared in those curious lists of the most influential thinkers, writers and consultants; lists that are the bread and butter of many business magazines.[2])

Throughout his life, Ackoff relied on the structure offered by Systems Thinking (an approach he did much to develop and popularise) to contain and shape his exciting and radical thinking. For anyone who knows Systems Thinking, this is no surprise. Amongst its other proponents are thought leaders like Margaret Mead, Buckminster Fuller, Abraham Maslow, Peter Drucker, W. Edwards Deming and

---

1   'Transforming the Systems Movement', given at the Third International Conference on Systems Thinking in Management (ICSTM '04).

2   See, for example, *Harvard Business Review*, December 2007.

Peter Senge. Through men and women like this, Systems Thinking has had a profoundly transformational effect on our world – not just the rarefied world of academic theorising but the practical world of government, education, town planning, architecture, organisational management, and so on. Even as I write, Systems Thinking has emerged once again at the top of the political agenda – this time in Britain where it forms the basis of Professor John Seddon's critique of the public sector and the culture of targets, inspection, economies of scale and much else besides.[3]

In this short book (which includes 40 new and previously unpublished f-Laws and is a companion to his original collection[4]), Russ Ackoff offers us more of his subversive wisdom about organisations – the unspoken laws and unconventional truths of management. But these f-Laws are much more than wicked epigrams; they are a distillation of his years of experience in developing and applying Systems Thinking.

We know that there are still many people at all levels of government and the public sector, as well as in finance, the service sector, industry and the third sector, who know nothing of Systems Thinking. Which is why we went to Russ with the idea of including this extended introduction to Systems Thinking – to help put in context his ideas on organisational issues like innovation, planning, creativity, corporate structure, salaries, performance measurement and much more.

First, let's pause to examine the standing of Systems Thinking in the world and to consider that assertion about the transformative effect of Systems Thinking.

---

3   See, for example, Andreas Whittam Smith's trenchant article on the public sector, 'A simple way to greater efficiency' in *The Independent*, 25th September, 2009.
4   *Management f-Laws*, Triarchy Press, 2007.

Systems Thinking caught in the cross-fire

As I've suggested, the stir[5] now being caused by John Seddon and others like him on the British political scene might lead an observer from Mars to suppose that Systems Thinking was a new idea. But, as the short list of 'big names' in the previous section suggests, it's been around the block a few times. So much so that Professor Fred Collopy (himself an advocate of Systems Thinking for more than three decades) wrote in his *Fast Company* blog[6] in June 2009 that Systems Thinking had been around for long enough and had failed to prove itself. Design Thinking,[7] he maintained, now needed to step into the shoes of Systems Thinking:

> *'Systems thinking, as written about and practiced by Russell Ackoff… and others, contained within it many of the impulses that motivate the application of design ideas to strategy, organization, society, and management… If the business and management community had bought it, we would not be having the many discussions about design, design thinking, and expanding management education to engage the intuitive, to embrace values, to look beyond available choices. We would already be doing all of that and more. But systems thinking… never really captured the imagination of business leaders. And we must learn from its mistakes.'*

Of course, his view is contentious and immediately provoked a riposte from Peter Jones in the *Integral Leadership Review.*[8] He argued that Systems Thinking couldn't be deemed to have failed since it (like a good number of sound theories before it) had never been systematically adopted. Blaming the time (and other) constraints faced by all senior executives he asked:

> *'What models do we purport or promote that an executive will be able to learn in one day and then retain in memory and experience for useful application?'*

---

5   See 'Walker v Seddon – the debate goes on' in *Local Government Chronicle,* 22nd July, 2009.

6   See http://tinyurl.com/lzh2p9 (accessed November 2009).

7   If you want to find out more about Design Thinking, a good place to start is Andrew Jones's *The Innovation Acid Test,* Triarchy Press, 2008.

8   *Integral Leadership Review,* Volume IX, No. 4 – August 2009.

He goes on to say:

> '*I have noticed that Professor Ackoff (or even I) can make a good theory work in practice, at least well enough to demonstrate its application. But can we expect management practitioners to follow our guidance, just from our writing management books and giving workshops?*'

Finally, he suggests that it doesn't really matter whether you call it Design Thinking or Systems Thinking. What needs to be done is for the theorists to move over and allow managers to 'bake theory into tangible practices'. He continues:

> '*The more these tools are employed in critical situations, the more they will be owned by the organization and not thought of as "thinking" practices at all. If we do our job well, the tools will become known by their local uses. They may become known as planning or collaboration practices. And we may again wonder whatever happened to "systems thinking".*'

But perhaps the most significant point to be made about all this comes from Jamshid Gharajedaghi. He reminds us in the Foreword that Ackoff himself was saying in 1974 that design would be the future of Systems methodology. If Russ Ackoff was happy to blend and interweave the two disciplines, then so can we be!

Still and all, Systems Thinking remains only slightly better known than its founding father, the Austrian Ludwig Von Bertalanffy[9]. And that's notwithstanding the fact that Peter Senge's most famous book (Systems Thinking *was* the eponymous fifth discipline) sold more than 2.5 million copies in its first edition alone. (Part of the explanation for that, of course, is that the spines on many of those 2.5 million books remain uncracked.)

So let's continue with our exploration of Systems Thinking in relation to just one area: management and the running of organisations, drawing on Russ Ackoff's f-Laws as well as earlier writings by both him and his colleagues. At the same time, let's bear in mind the conviction of Ackoff and many others that Systems Thinking works and Peter Jones' reminder (above) that Systems *Thinking* is seldom seen because it is so often hiding behind other, effective, *practices*.

---

9   The International Society for the Systems Sciences has a good introduction to him at www.isss.org/lumLVB.htm

Definitions

So what is Systems Thinking when applied to management and to work in general? It's perhaps easiest to start with conventional thinking. Our habit (in the West, at least) has for a long time been take any complex system (like a business), separate it out into its component parts and then try to understand and manage each part as well as possible.[10] Parts could here refer to different departments or work processes or products or individuals. If that's done, the theory goes, the system as a whole will behave well.

[The boxed numbers here and elsewhere refer to specific f-Laws that expand on a specific idea. You will find numbers 1-81 summarized in this book starting on page 33 and explained in detail in *Management f-Laws*. Numbers 82 onwards are published for the first time in this volume, starting on page 39.]

The problem is that it's perfectly possible to understand or improve the function or performance of one part (even many parts) and yet to misunderstand, disable or even destroy the system as a whole at the same time. There are many examples of this in Ackoff's writing:

75

In terms of understanding, Ackoff would ask us to consider how a complete appreciation of all the working parts of an automobile don't help to understand why it is that Americans drive on the right side and Britons on the wrong side of the road.

In terms of improvement, Ackoff would ask us to consider how DDT helped control malaria and yellow fever, how Thalidomide helped treat anxiety and insomnia, how oil has powered extraordinary improvement in the quality of life of millions of people – and then consider the wider picture.

Or let's look at education. Every school child soon learns that, when they're asked a question, they first need to decide what answer is expected. This approach is a recipe for continuously improving exam results but it is not a recipe for creative and original thinking.

24

---

10   See, for example, Peter Day's discussion of Fordism in his February 2007 article on Ackoff's f-Laws at the BBC website (http://news.bbc.co.uk/1/hi/business/6338527. stm) and 'Facilitating Systemic Thinking in Business Classes' in *Decision Sciences: Journal of Innovative Education*, Volume 4, No. 2, 2006.

It is Russ Ackoff's contention that most organisations and most managers are similarly hampered. For all the talk of innovation in business, most organisations still systematically discourage innovative thinking. (Again, the f-Laws later in this book offer numerous examples.)

17

But I digress already. Let's try a working definition of Systems Thinking:

> **Systems thinking looks at relationships (rather than unrelated objects), connectedness, process (rather than structure), the whole (rather than just its parts), the patterns (rather than the contents) of a system, and context.**

86

> **Thinking systemically also requires several shifts in perception, which lead in turn to different ways to teach, and different ways to organise society.**

That definition includes 'the whole rather than just the parts', which we have just discussed briefly, but much more besides.

So let's go back a step and just check what a system is. As Bill Bellows (Russ Ackoff's one-time student and, later, his respected colleague) elegantly puts it:

> *'A system is a set or pattern of relationships that work together in some fashion. Systems can accomplish things that would be impossible if the same elements were put into random relationships, or no relationships at all…*
>
> *'Although we may sometimes take it for granted, we get enormous value from systems every day. We benefit continually from various smart puttings-together of resources that provide us with food, transportation, education, goods and services…'*[11]

So, as well as emphasising the importance of seeing the whole rather than the parts, we obviously need to focus on relationships and communication between those parts, on what Bill calls puttings-together and on the things that strengthen or weaken those relationships.

112

---

11 The extract is from notes supplied to me by Bill Bellows, who is a remarkable Systems Thinker and Associate Technical Fellow and Lead, Enterprise Thinking Network at Pratt & Whitney Rocketdyne. For more about him and his ideas, see http://in2in.org

The Feedback Loop

Let us begin with what strengthens and weakens relationships. We start with what are popularly known as vicious circles and virtuous circles – terms that more or less started life with Systems Thinking. One of the most interesting terms used in Systems Thinking is the technical term for those circles: the feedback loop.[12]

In *The Dueling Loops of the Political Powerplace*,[13] Jack Harich explains – in words of several syllables but in sentences that make complete sense – how feedback loops work in politics. Specifically, he explains why it is that politicians and the global political-economic system have failed to address 'the environmental problem' for the last 30 years (and particularly since the Rio Convention of 1992).

Two races: to the bottom and to the top

The core of Harich's argument is the idea that, in democratic politics, two races can take place. They're the race to the top and the race to the bottom. The race to the bottom is characterised by the use of falsehood and favouritism. (Harich calls the two, together, 'corruption'.) When this strategy prevails, politicians make false and/or unfeasible promises, they play on fear and create scapegoats (terrorism, communism, liberalism, etc.), they campaign using half-truths and generalities and they rely on support that is bought or rewarded with political favours. In the race to the top, politicians will, by contrast, confront the truth and the harsh realities of any situation, they will make honest assessments of their motivations and their ability to achieve change, they will make realistic undertakings and they will appoint the best people for the job regardless of what favours they may owe.

122

Now these two models are not particularly new. For a long time, commentators have deplored the race to the bottom and the role that the mass media play in that race. Again and again, we have seen politicians apparently setting out on a race to the top (Bill Clinton and Tony Blair come quickly to mind) but getting diverted or diverting to a strategy that more often uses falsehood and favouritism.

---

12 I have not discussed the important distinction between positive and negative feedback loops here. They are well worth reading more about.

13 The paper is online at www.thwink.org

What is important to notice is that both strategies are feedback loops. In the case of falsehood, the race to the bottom depends on those falsehoods being spread about widely, being taken up and becoming accepted. The theory talks of these falsehoods as memes and suggests that the population becomes 'infected' with them.[14] As more people are infected, the falsehoods gain more credibility and they are spread more widely. The weight of opinion gradually shifts. The role of the media is central here.

Of course, political leaders themselves are implicated in this loop. It is probably rare for 'race to the top' politicians to wake up one day and choose deliberately to race to the bottom instead. It's more likely that, under pressure, on the defensive and advised by pragmatic 'courtiers', they will resort to a white lie here or there. The support of a key player may be bought on one occasion 'for the greater good' and so on. The demands of the 'powerplace' invite politicians to compromise and realpolitik offers seductive and effective ways for politicians to get the job done.

26

If the politicians are buoyed up by a wave of popular support, we – their supporters – will also be caught up in the loop. We will look the other way and refuse to acknowledge what is happening until gradually, repulsed by what is going on, we become part of a new feedback loop characterised by disillusion and disenchantment and we seek a new political leader on whom to bestow our faith.

We've been talking here about politics, but Systems Thinking tells us that the principles underlying the operation of one sociosystem will be pretty much like those underpinning another. So we can look to organisations and expect to find something similar happening. And, sure enough, we can recognise – beside those who clearly set out on the path of corruption – that many organisational leaders drift into the race to the bottom, espousing falsehood and favouritism and relying more on packaging, presentation and PR than on lived values and 'walking the talk'.

55

And what is true of organisational leaders is also true of the organisations themselves and the culture espoused by staff or members of the organisation. (Perhaps it was a tacit recognition of this fact that led Google to adopt the

66

---

14   See, for example, www.thedailymeme.com or Richard Dawkins' *The Selfish Gene* if you want to know more about memes.

disingenuously simplistic 'Don't be evil' motto. And perhaps it is a tacit recognition of the same fact by the media that results in commentators hovering round the Googleplex like vultures, determined to show that Google's policies on scanning the world's books or storing and using customer data are in breach of that same motto.)

Tropisms

We've just seen that, often, when a politician shifts from the race to the top to the race to the bottom, this may not be a simple act or a clear, conscious decision. It 'happens' and we are all caught up in it. This notion of how things come about is also central to Systems Thinking and it's not just confined to politics.

In *Towards the Third Modernity*,[15] his masterful analysis of social change over the last sixty years, Alain de Vulpian (a Systems Thinker to the core) is careful to talk always of tropisms rather than trends. Why? Because he clearly sees societal changes as co-created. We may want them to happen or they may seem somehow to 'insist' on happening. But, in the end, neither of those things is enough on its own. It needs both. Take the arrival of the mobile phone. Early adopters seized them with delight. But most of the rest of the population mocked them at first, laughed at people who used them, said they'd never have one, got one grudgingly for emergencies, began to use it, came to depend on it, complained that it could work better, said they'd never use one with a camera, upgraded to one that does more, used it as a camera *in extremis*, etc.

This process was not conjured up by the mobile phone companies and their marketing wizards alone. The technology fed a desire, the desire became a demand, the demand became consciously articulated, use created further demand, tipping points were reached, and new technology tantalised. Consumers, media and producers were all complicit and implicated in the way the mobile phone took our world by storm. The process emerged and happened and we turned our heads to listen to the incoming call as a field of French sunflowers turns to face the sun.

91

The key to the process probably lies somewhere in those 'plic' words – complicit and implicit – which suggest that the process is folded over and over like a brain. Those folds allow for gaps to be jumped, short cuts to be found and multiple paths to be followed. And we'll find more plic words, as well as plex words (plex being the root from which the plic grows) as we go on: complexity, duplicity, multiplicity, and so on.

15   Triarchy Press, 2008.

Incidentally, there are multiple implications from this discussion of tropisms for marketing and organisational performance and Russ Ackoff points out many of them. He reminds us that the counterintuitive answer is often the right one:

- As consumers, we'll pay more for things we don't need than for things we do need.

  93

- The more corporate directors are paid, the smaller their contribution is likely to be.

  77

- The amount spent by an organisation on a commercial is inversely related to its truth and relevance.

  44

- The less managers understand their business, the more variables they require to explain it.

  21

Self-Organisation

As well as talking of tropisms, Vulpian also talks of the *auto-organisation* – meaning a self-organising organisation. This raises the whole question of what we mean by an organisation. Most definitions have it as some kind of ordered coming-together (or putting-together, as Bill Bellows might say) of multiple elements with the intention of achieving some aim more effectively than any or all of those elements could manage on their own.

Clearly, any definition like this suggests that an organisation is a system and is going to be susceptible to Systems Thinking. One way of talking about an organisation or a system in this way is to say that a system is *not* like a mound of sand. Take away a few grains and not much changes except that the pile gets a little smaller. Instead, imagine a system as a car. Take away a headlight and it works less well. Take away a spark plug or the carburettor and the system rapidly ceases to function as it was designed (though it may become a good place to seek shelter from a sandstorm or to grow strawberries).

Still, a mechanical metaphor like this can seem a bit too static. It doesn't properly represent the dynamic interconnectedness of the elements of a system. A biological metaphor may be better. Let us think of the human body as a system (von Bertalanffy was a biologist, by the way) and it reminds us that the kidney sends signals to the brain, just as the brain sends signals to the kidney. Furthermore, the human body as a system is normally self-regulating, so it adapts to and affects the surrounding environment – it is part of a nexus of systems.

119

But while it is progress to see any system – and specifically an organisation – as a biological organism, it is not enough. It enables us to concentrate on the whole system rather than on the parts. But, in a biological organism the parts (take the kidney again) have no function other than to serve the organism as a whole. This isn't true of an organisation. So we need to see the organisation as a social system, like a village or a society. We need to see it as a community. This has implications: a community doesn't have owners; individual community members have lives and intentions and needs just as much as the community as a whole; and authority (if those of us who are democrats are to be consistent with our political principles) must flow from the bottom up – by election. There are many points here to explore further. But let's return for now to Vulpian's description of a self-organising organisation.

That is to say a more or less loosely structured grouping or association, often coming together in response to a perceived injustice or problem, usually structured on heterarchical[16] principles and deliberately avoiding the formal rules, regulations and chains of command to be found in a conventional organisation. Vulpian sees the wired (now wireless) world as characterised by these self-organisations (which are, in turn, facilitated by the Internet, social media and networking technology and applications of all sorts).

He sees the world as teetering on the edge of a radical shift towards more self-organisation and towards a more responsible and engaged approach to our fellow humans and the planet – a shift that could be encouraged or prevented by climatic, geopolitical or other extreme events.

For Russ Ackoff, the implications of this self-making, self-organising characteristic of systems are more immediate. Most importantly, he was in the habit of saying that we (managers, leaders, planners) often make things worse by our interventions. For example:

- Greed at senior levels results in inequities and inefficiencies throughout an organisation

  84/5

- Internal monopolies result in distortion, incompetence and further inefficiency.

  111

- Mergers and acquisitions are, as a rule, counter-productive.

  39

Whether or not we are optimistic about the emergence of self-organising solutions to the planet's problems, we can clearly see that this way of viewing the world has deep roots in Systems Thinking. This perspective is significantly extended in the Systems Thinking approach by an idea called autopoiesis. So named by

---

16 Heterarchy suggests a more distributed, networked, heterogeneous, flat, multi-centred distribution of authority than is found in a hierarchy.

Maturana and Varela,[17] the theory of autopoiesis proposes that the system not only organises itself but literally makes itself. The implication of this is that the system and, in this case, the organisation, has a life of its own.

This is echoed in many extensions of Systems Thinking: complexity theorist Lesley Kuhn, for example, talks of 'the life of organisations' rather than just 'organisations', while Systems Thinker and consultant Bill Tate has built on the work of Gerald Egan in talking about the 'shadow side' of the organisation. This theory suggests that the organisation operates in a way like the individual human psyche, with certain topics, feelings, drives and intentions being 'out of bounds', unmentionable or even 'unconscious' in both the individual and the organisation.

One example of this 'unconsciousness' in organisations can be found in Ackoff's analysis of knowledge. In an approach much followed by researchers in the field of knowledge management, he asserts that there are two sorts of knowledge: implicit and explicit. Implicit or tacit knowledge is what organisations and people in them know without thinking. This knowledge is hard to unearth, hard to transmit and hard to store.

2

One of the implications of feedback loops, tropisms, autopoiesis and self-organisation is that everything is connected. To be clear that this is not a simple (simplex!) process, we can say that everything is interconnected.

---

17   *Autopoiesis and Cognition*, Kluwer, 1980.

Interconnectedness

The first thing to say about interconnectedness is that:

> *'no-one is directing this system of connections and interconnections.*
> *Those who are involved have no clear idea of the effect of their actions*
> *on the system as a whole and even the most powerful social actors can*
> *at most only temporarily deflect a process which will eventually bypass*
> *them or carry them with it'.*[18]

This is a reminder of what we were looking at in the previous section: that political and organisational leaders are probably less in control of things than they imagine. Things self-organise. What happens next in any system is an emergent property of everything that has gone before. This is probably bad news for conspiracy theorists. But it's also bad news for anyone wedded to the idea that using a hierarchy is the most efficient way of getting things done.

Hierarchies are vulnerable in all sorts of ways: to breaks in communication and the chain of command; to attack (witness the threats to British and American forces in Afghanistan when their operating procedures are discovered by the Taliban); to subversion (from discontented or malicious elements within the hierarchy); to stupidity (when someone unthinkingly 'just obeys orders'); to creativity ('oh god, someone's been using their initiative again).

Heterarchical networks, on the other hand, are much more resilient; instructions can get through via multiple channels; they are based on goodwill rather than fear; they set out to foster creativity; and so on. All this has been explained at length by Gerard Fairtlough, who points the finger of blame at what he calls 'the hegemony of hierarchy' – the widely-held belief that hierarchy is the only way of getting things done efficiently or at all.[19] (The belief is based on many things: our upbringing, the way society has worked for a long time, the way almost all significant institutions work and our genetic roots. But, Gerard argues, just because hens have a pecking order and dogs have cringing behaviours and chimpanzees have their alpha males, doesn't mean that we have to go on doing that stuff. By the same

---

18   I'm quoting Alain de Vulpian again.
19   See *The Three Ways of Getting Things Done,* Triarchy Press, 2007.

token, bank voles, wolf spiders and other creatures eat their young, but humans have largely stopped doing so. Shift happens.)

Of course, what underlies the possibility of a move from hierarchy to a cooperative, heterarchical network is the arrival of trust. Hierarchical command-and-control systems by and large operate on the basis that everything can be traced back and checked up on. They assume very little trust. Cooperative systems dispense with the stick, checks and controls and rely on trust. No surprise then that the last book written by Gerard Fairtlough (who ran big businesses, including Shell Chemicals UK and Celltech, so knew what he was talking about) was called *No Secrets: Innovation through Openness*. What underpins openness? Trust.[20]

So it's the feedback loops and the interconnected structure itself that make the system work in this interconnected way of thinking.

While we're on the subject of things self-organising and 'what happens next', we need to think about what *does* happen next. 'In the wild', what happens next is that the system begins to mature, reaches maturity, becomes over-ripe or over-blown, and eventually – having dropped its fruit, sent out suckers, produced more tubers or laid its eggs – dies. Arie de Geus's ground-breaking book *The Living Organisation*[21] started life as a piece of research into organisational longevity – why was it, the author wondered, that the average multinational company had a lifespan of only forty years? What characterised those that lasted longer? What enabled a tiny few to survive for centuries? The short answer, of course, has to do with entropy. Living things get old and die. Decay happens. Order reverts gradually to chaos.[22] In any case, Systems Thinking has plenty to say about ageing and Russ Ackoff is particularly trenchant in his critical analysis of the way in which senior management handle the process of organisational maturation.

| 82 |

---

20 The acknowledged expert on trust in business is Ackoff's collaborator Sally Bibb. See *A Question of Trust*, Cyan Communications, 2007.

21 Harvard Business School Press and Nicholas Brealey Publishing, 1997.

22 The theory of entropy has been much challenged and its challengers challenged. Perhaps it's all a question of perspective. Is the disintegration and degeneration of an untended garden (reverting from 'order' to 'chaos') actually a reversion to the natural order and balance represented by a wild field – in whose lifespan the brief time it has spent as an artificially ordered garden is simply a disordered aberration?

He also reminds us of something overlooked but obvious: that change makes much of what was learned in the past irrelevant or obsolete. Learning to drive a car doesn't equip me to drive a spaceship. Experience is no longer the best teacher. Which is one reason why longevity is no advantage to an organisation. This principle is also related to Ackoff's understanding of the role of inertia in organisations: 'the only thing harder than starting something new is stopping something old'.

6

19

Equifinality

All this interconnectedness and all these feedback loops mean that there isn't really a top or bottom to any structure when seen in Systems Thinking terms. Which is alarming for people who are used to the idea of giving an order and getting it implemented. (But then the world is alarming for people like that. If you've ever worked in an organisation that's been subject to a culture change initiative, you'll know that they rarely work. And they never work unless they can win over 'hearts and minds'.) For Systems Thinkers, the way to make a big change is to start with a very small change or 'input' and just see what happens.

That input can have all sorts of unpredictable and interconnected effects. Different feedback loops can be set in motion. Everything else happening in the organisation will feed into this 'disruption' and eventually you can identify an outcome (although any particular outcome is actually just a staging post on the way to yet further outcomes). The point of equifinality is that it highlights the fact that there are multiple routes to the same destination.

This idea of making just a very small change is one of the numerous overlaps between Systems Thinking and complexity theory (another plex) and its sibling, chaos theory. That small institutional change is the Systems Thinking equivalent of the now-famous butterfly (for some reason normally located somewhere in the Pacific) flapping its wings nonchalantly and unwittingly precipitating a tornado in South Dakota.[23]

---

23 This theme is taken up by Graham Leicester and Maureen O'Hara in *Ten Things to Do in a Conceptual Emergency* (IFF Publications, 2009), where their tenth thing (Practise Social Acupuncture) is based on the fact that 'even a small disturbance, artfully designed, can have large systemic effects'. Likewise, Occupational Therapist Simon Curle compares the role of an OT to that of a tiny, well-positioned marble, which through leverage can bring about a relatively major shift in the position or movement of two huge boulders.

Events vs. systems

Interconnectedness, equifinality and tropisms are just a few of the things that tend to sabotage the causal – or, more precisely, linear-causal – way in which we are used to thinking. Take crime. Politicians are aware that for most people (often including themselves) crime has a cause. If we want to solve crime, we have to find the cause and fix it. That could mean deciding that deterrents are not strong enough and increasing prison sentences. Or that there aren't enough police and hiring more. Or even that young criminals don't have enough hobbies and opening more youth clubs.

But, essentially, it's people's misbehaviour that is seen to cause the problem. The solution is to get people to stop committing crimes. Usually they decide that this is best done with new laws. But history tells us that this approach doesn't usually work.

Systems Thinkers see things differently. People's behaviour is down to a whole series of interconnections and multiple causes and feedback loops. It's the system that causes people to commit crimes (perhaps through a combination of huge imbalances in the distribution of wealth, differential access to good education and high levels of unemployment) and the system that has to be fixed.

Now any thoughtful person knows that we need to look at the broader picture in this way when we're considering society and social problems. But this kind of thinking hasn't really filtered through to smaller organisations (or sociosystems as Systems Thinkers call them) like companies or government bodies and agencies or NGOs. That means that senior managers who are aware of the notion of complex, multiple causation in society at large are still prone to imagining that a single or simple cause can be found to explain a logistics problem or a persistent customer service breakdown. Probably it can't. And Russ Ackoff also had strong views on this kind of simplistic, unimaginative thinking.

80

According to Ackoff, because most managers don't have the knowledge and understanding that are needed to deal with complexity, they try to reduce complex situations to simple ones. This has several consequences: they look for statistics and measures that will give them simple answers; they look for simple solutions to problems; and they turn to consultants and gurus who present quick fixes and simple cures.

51

Parts vs. the whole

You remember that Systems Thinking likes to look at the whole rather than at the parts? We all know that's a good idea. But it still often gets forgotten in the heat of the moment. Take that customer service breakdown or a profit shortfall: managers turn into inspectors, breaking down the process into its component parts to see where it went wrong, or breaking down the business into its cost/profit centres to see which to cut and which to keep. Scapegoats are found. Blame is apportioned.

In Ackoff's seeing, 'parts management' – that is to say managerial decisions made by and for individual units in isolation from the other units – is the norm in today's organisation. This foments competition, often fierce, between units for increasingly scarce resources. Decisions taken in concert with other departments or units, a process that benefits the whole as well as the parts because each part learns what it can do together with the others to advance the whole, are the exception.

| 3 |

But remember the feedback loops. Cause and effect is not simple and linear. Social systems (and organisations are social systems) are complex and their behaviour is complex and difficult to predict. Different effects manifest themselves over different lengths of time. Peter Senge used the famous example of a company that cuts back on advertising, sees the benefits of reduced costs, cuts again, sees more benefits, and so on until, too late, an analyst notices the impact of the declining number of new customers.[24]

---

24 This is taken from the section on feedback in *The Fifth Discipline*, Doubleday, 1990.

The whole in context

Of mounting importance in Systems Thinking is the idea of ecological thinking, a connection that we can reasonably attribute to Gregory Bateson.[25] Just as all the component or process parts of the organisation or system are interrelated in multiple, complex ways, so the organisation as a whole – and its parts – are intricately related and correlated with the surrounding environment. Of course this means the physical environment, but also the social environment, the market environment, the cultural environment and the competitive, organisational environment.

Everything the organisation and its component parts and its individual members do has an effect on the surrounding environment. That's environmental thinking. But beyond that, the organisation is a dynamic, (constantly changing) aggregation of people and processes operating in (or, actually, cooperating with) its dynamic (constantly changing) surroundings. There is no starting point in Systems Thinking. There is always movement and there is always flow. We have always already started.[26]

[If this is starting to sound alarming, that may be because of the way that we are taught to think in the West. Sinologist and philosopher François Jullien has recently published a book[27] that explains how Chinese thinking (both philosophical and quotidian) tends to value transition, transformation, modification, adaptation, process and flow, while Western thinking (and he means the classical Greek approach to which we are the heirs) tends to stress state, status, boundary and clear definition. For example, science in the West will usually seek to determine and categorise (is this snow or water, solid or liquid?), while Chinese thinking will be more comfortable with the idea that this slush is moving along a continuum.]

---

25 See his *Steps to an Ecology of Mind*, University of Chicago Press, 1972.

26 My understanding of the ecological movement and of the relationship of ecological thinking to Systems Thinking begins with the work of Sandra Reeve: www.moveintolife.co.uk/EcologicalBody/

27 *Les transformations silencieuses*, Grasset, 2009.

Recognising this contextual interconnectedness is ecological thinking. And Gregory Bateson (above) neatly summarises the issue when he says in *Steps to an Ecology of Mind*:

> *'The major problems in the world are the result of the difference between how nature works and the way people think.'*[28]

---

28   If you want to know more at once, you will find a film and many other materials about Bateson at www.anecologyofmind.com

Mess

The culmination of System Thinking's approach to ecological thinking, interconnectedness and complex, multiple causality is that Systems Thinkers adopt a complex approach to the *mess* that I quoted Russ Ackoff talking about at the beginning of this introduction. As his late friend and colleague Sheldon Rovin says:

> 'What do I mean by "mess?" The "mess" I am talking about is not what happens when you spill something on a floor or on your lap. It's not about what your infant child does in her diaper. The "mess" I mean is not a single problem. I use "mess" to represent an interacting set of problems, a system of problems, that won't be solved by any simple, single, narrow focus. The world's problems are an interacting, inextricably connected cluster of disorders that thus far have eluded either resolution or solution, chiefly because they are approached as single or isolated concerns.'[29]

The nature of the *mess* (complex and interconnected, weblike) means that any process or mechanism for cleaning up the *mess* must be similarly weblike. Here again we find Russ Ackoff had strong opinions about the simplistic type of solution offered by consultants, taught to Business School students and sought by most managers.

18

40

A significant conclusion drawn by Ackoff is that, faced with a problem: *you can't do just one thing.* You can't change only one thing and expect to accomplish anything substantial on behalf of an entire system.

---

29   From the first draft of a book on Systems Thinking submitted to us by Sheldon in 2008.

Analysis vs. synthesis

According to Ackoff and other Systems Thinkers, conventional thinking is based on analysis – breaking things down into their constituent parts, seeking to understand the behaviour of those parts and then deducing rules and principles about the behaviour of the whole system from the behaviour of its parts. Systems Thinking uses synthesis and synthetic thinking to do the exact opposite – to understand and explain the whole system and the interactions between its parts.

There are many corollaries for a Systems Thinker. Here are just three:

- Development is more important and beneficial than growth.

  54

This is an extension of the pile of sand analogy. Growth just makes a system bigger and, like dinosaurs, often less efficient and more vulnerable. Development makes a system better able to do what it was designed or intended to do.

- Doing the right thing is more important than doing the thing right, especially if that thing is the wrong thing.

  109

This idea is often attributed to Peter Drucker, another Systems Thinker. It doesn't matter who started it. It remains a crucial test of any business strategy or – at a smaller level – of any activity or task that you're about to undertake.

- Starting with the ideal situation/product rather than the existing one is the better way to design anything.

  4

This approach is called 'idealised design'. It is usually credited to Russ Ackoff and is the subject of two of his books: *Idealized Design*[30] and *Redesigning Society*[31] (the latter written with Sheldon Rovin). Sheldon characterised[32] the approach as follows:

---

30   Wharton School Publishing, 2006.
31   Stanford University Press, 2003.
32   In the draft manuscript mentioned on page 23.

'A design process that enables the constraint-free use of our brains is called idealized design. It was developed by Russell Ackoff, my mentor and sometimes tormentor… Idealized design is a systems based way of thinking about a future that you want now, not one you have to settle for or is given to you by others or is off in the future. It is a learning based way of planning that helps you be creative and generate alternatives. It can enable you to conceive the inconceivable and to come up with ideas that no other way of thinking that I know of can. It does this by taking you back to the thinking of your childhood, when anything and everything was possible because as a child you weren't worried by constraints.'

Failure to learn

An obvious question for anyone reading about Systems Thinking
(and one that Ackoff was often asked) is why, given what a
thoroughly good theory it is, more organisations have not adopted
Systems Thinking.[33]

We have already discussed the number of unread copies of Peter
Senge's *The Fifth Discipline*, but Ackoff suggested other
reasons.[34] His 'general reason' for the failure of
organisations to learn from their mistakes is that there are

> 116

two sorts of mistake: visible errors of commission and the
insidiously invisible errors of omission. The latter (things we did not
do and should have done) are seldom caught by company
audits or reporting systems, rarely acknowledged and
almost never learnt from. They are connected to the 'mind

> 101

your back' approach to management and decision-making
characterised by the idea that the chief preoccupation of most
managers is the avoidance of risk. Ackoff attributed these
shortfalls in learning, risk-taking and initiative to our
educational system.

> 99

The second and more particular reason that he gave is that
Systems Thinkers do not talk clearly or effectively to
practising managers. They largely talk to one another in an
academic enclave. He maintained that they have painted
themselves into a box and are unable to think out of it.

> 61

A third reason has to do with the nature of work and our
approach to learning, careers, promotion and retirement.
As Ackoff said elsewhere:

> 1

> *'As an executive's professional future approaches zero, there appears
> to be nothing new under the sun and, therefore, nothing new worth
> trying. In other words the future increasingly comes to be seen as a
> repetition of the past.'*

---

33 Here we come back to the issue raised by Professor Collopy and discussed on
    page 3.
34 Presented in 'Why few organizations adopt systems thinking', which can be read
    at http://ackoffcenter.blogs.com

A fourth reason is that System Thinking challenges paradigms. It can often seem controversial and uncomfortable as it challenges our usual ways of seeing the world and of seeing the organisations that we work in. This little volume and its companion book, *Management f-Laws*, are an illustration of exactly that. Almost all of the f-Laws take some generally accepted principle of business and turn it on its head. In the process they highlight the fact that many organisations and many senior managers are continuing to flog more than one dead horse (believing that customers know best, that information is useful in decision-making, that solving a problem is not usually the best thing to do with it, and so on).

87

As an aside, Sheldon Rovin in his first draft of a guide to Systems Thinking, repeated this old chestnut:

> *The often-quoted tribal wisdom of the Dakota Indians, passed on from generation to generation, says that, 'When you discover that you are riding a dead horse, the best strategy is to dismount.' However, in government more advanced strategies are often employed, such as:*

1. *Buying a stronger whip.*
2. *Changing riders.*
3. *Appointing a committee to study the horse.*
4. *Arranging to visit other countries to see how other cultures ride horses.*

29

5. *Lowering the standards so that dead horses can be included.*
6. *Reclassifying the dead horse as living impaired.*
7. *Hiring outside contractors to ride the dead horse.*
8. *Harnessing several dead horses together to increase speed.*

82

9. *Providing extra funding/training to increase the dead horse's performance.*
10. *Doing a productivity study to see if lighter riders would improve the dead horse's performance.*
11. *Declaring that as the dead horse does not have to be fed, it is less costly, carries lower overhead and therefore contributes substantially more to the bottom line of the economy than live horses.*

3

12. Rewriting the expected performance requirements for all horses. And, of course...

13. Promoting the dead horse to a supervisory position.

Change

The flip-side of failure to learn is successful change and Russ Ackoff always had much to say about how to achieve that desirable state of affairs from a Systems Thinking perspective.

His first rule is based on the principles of idealised design, which we met earlier. It simply suggests working backwards from where you want to be – an obvious but often overlooked solution. This applies both to the practical management of change and to the conceptual journey that precedes it.

| 89 |
| 90 |

Perhaps more surprisingly, Ackoff had little time for the practices of continuous improvement and benchmarking which governed much of the drive for business excellence in the West over the last 25 years. His objection to them was that they are slow, imitative not creative, limiting, and condemn the organisation to follower status. Enough said!

| 96 |
| 97 |

Finally, Systems Thinking tells us that, because organisations are complex, immeasurable and unpredictable things, science can only help us so far when it comes to planning change. In the end, as Ackoff says, 'the quality of their intuitions differentiates managers more than the quality of what they know and understand'.

| 110 |

Aims and intentions

I talked earlier about openness, intentions and the 'shadow side' of the organisation. This was a theme that Ackoff often returned to in discussing change management in the organisation.

When you're setting out to change things in an organisation, he said, you need to look at the organisation's aims and objectives. As Ackoff observed,[35] the ones that must be changed are not usually those that are proclaimed in public mission statements; rather they are the ones that are actually pursued. For example, while most corporations proclaim maximisation of shareholder value as their primary objective, this is often an illusion. The principal objective of corporations is to maximise the security, standard of living, and quality of life of those making the decisions. As he said at the time, 'Recent disclosures at Enron and WorldCom, among others, made this abundantly clear'.

58

A similar discrepancy between objective proclaimed and objective practised can be observed in most organisations. For example, one could mistakenly believe that the principal objective of universities is to educate students. But for Ackoff, the principal objective of a university is to provide job security and increase the standard of living and quality of life of those members of the faculty and administration who make the critical decisions. Teaching is the price that faculty members must pay to share in the benefits provided. Like any price, they try to minimise it. Note that the more senior and politically powerful teaching members of the faculty are, the less teaching they do.

117

Here and elsewhere, Ackoff's harshest criticism was always reserved for a system that he himself was a part of: the higher education system. But, characteristically, even prolific authors like himself were not spared:

115

> *'Oh, and by the way, no author has ever read all the books he or she cites.'*

---

35   In *Transforming the Systems Movement,* at
     www.acasa.upenn.edu/RLAConfPaper.pdf

People

All this talk of systems and self-organisation can tend to discourage
talk of individuals. Systems Thinking says that, as a rule, in
the event of a serious problem it's the system that's at fault,
not any one individual. Equally, Ackoff and Systems
Thinking tend to downplay the role of individual
executives and leaders in shaping or directing the future of
a company, in making profits or in doing anything very much.

42

Nonetheless, organisations are full of people and what they do
matters. Ackoff famously observed one of the shifts that occurred in
the workplace during the 20th century. At the start of it, 95%
(say) of employees could not do their job as well as their
boss could. (In other words, the foreman would typically
be more experienced in using the lathe than was the lathe
operative.) By the end, 95% of employees could do their job
better than their boss could.

5

There are many reasons for this, including the arrival of all kinds of
new technology, the need for one person to manage many people
with many different specialised skills, the growth of a whole range
of service-related skills, the increased value of human relationships
with individual customers. In this situation, Ackoff realised that
you cannot manage what people do any more. You can only hope to
manage they way they interact and how they relate to one another.

In conclusion

In these and his other f-Laws, Russ Ackoff ranges even more widely than this introduction to some of the principles of Systems Thinking would suggest. He was an extraordinarily eclectic thinker, happily able to cover problem-solving, innovation, organisational structures, managers' bad habits and training, to name but a few, in a single, deft paragraph. Most of his f-Laws share that quality of all good insights – they make you say, 'Of course, why didn't I see that before, it's obvious!'. And all of them bring us back, directly or indirectly, to the principles outlined here.

In this book, and throughout his professional life, Russ Ackoff made a point of showing that Systems Thinking attracts related ideas and techniques precisely because it offers such a robust and comprehensive theory of how organisations work.

But read on and find for yourself what insights Systems Thinking and Russ Ackoff have brought and can continue to bring to the world of work. And see the Additional Reading section at the end of the book if you'd like to take it any further.

If you're hoping to find insights that may help you instigate or bring about change in your organisation, remember one of the first rules of Systems Thinking:

> *'Don't fight the system, change the rules and the system will change itself.'*

Andrew Carey

andrew@triarchypress.com

P.S. A reminder that the boxed numbers in the preceding text refer to specific f-Laws that expand on a specific idea. The bare bones of numbers 1-81 are reprinted on the next few pages, but the full explanation and commentary appears only in *Management f-Laws*. The remaining f-Laws (number 82 onwards) start on page 39 of this book.

Management f-Laws numbers 1-81

1.   You can't teach an old dog or executive new tricks, or even that there *are* any new tricks

2.   Knowledge is of two types, explicit and implicit, and knowing this is implicit

3.   You rarely improve an organisation as a whole by improving the performance of one or more of its parts

4.   There is no point in asking consumers, who do not know what they want, to say what they want

5.   All managers believe they can do their boss's job better than their boss can, but they forget that their subordinates share the same belief about themselves

6.   For managers the only conditions under which experience is the best teacher are ones in which no change takes place

7.   The level of conformity in an organisation is in inverse proportion to its creative ability

8.   The best reason for recording what one thinks is to discover what one thinks and to organise it in transmittable form

9.   No corporation should retain a business unit that is worth more outside the corporation than within it

10. The amount of irrationality that executives attribute to others is directly proportional to their own

11. The future is better dealt with using assumptions than forecasts

12. An organisation's planning horizon is the same as its CEO's retirement horizon

13. The lower the rank of managers, the more they know about fewer things. The higher the rank of managers, the less they know about many things

14.   The importance of executives is directly proportional to the size of their waiting rooms and the number of intervening secretaries

15.   When managers say something is obvious, it does not mean that it is unquestionable, but rather that they are unwilling to have it questioned

16.   The less sure managers are of their opinions, the more vigorously they defend them

17.   The more lawyers an organisation employs, the less innovation it tolerates

18.   Good teachers produce sceptics who ask their own questions and find their own answers; management gurus produce only unquestioning disciples

19.   The only thing more difficult than starting something new in an organisation is stopping something old

20.   Acceptance of a recommended solution to a problem depends more on the manager's trust of its source than on the content of the recommendation or the competence of its source

21.   The less managers understand their business, the more variables they require to explain it

22.   The higher the rank of managers, the less is the distance between their offices and their restrooms

23.   Business schools are as difficult to change as cemeteries, and for the same reasons

24.   Curiosity is the 'open sesame' to learning, even for managers

25.   The legibility of a male manager's handwriting is in inverse proportion to his seniority

26.   Executives must be prevented from receiving any information about frauds or immoral acts committed by their subordinates

27.   There is nothing that a manager wants done that educated subordinates cannot undo

28.   The more corporate executives believe in a free (unregulated) market, the more they believe in a regulated internal market

29.   The amount of time a committee wastes is directly proportional to its size

30.   It is generally easier to evaluate an organisation from the outside-in than from the inside-out

31.   Development is less about how much an organisation has than how much it can do with whatever it has

32.   Smart subordinates can make their managers look bad no matter how good they are, and make their managers look good no matter how bad they are

33.   In an organisation that disapproves of mistakes, but identifies only errors of commission, the best strategy for anyone who seeks job security is to do nothing

34.   The best organisational designers are ones who know how to beat any organisation designed by others

35.   The offence taken by an organisation from negative press is directly proportional to its truthfulness

36.   The less important an issue is, the more time managers spend discussing it

37.   The time spent waiting to get into an executive's office is directly proportional to the difference in rank between the executive and the one waiting to get in

38.   Administration, management and leadership are not the same thing

39.   In acquisitions the value added to the acquired company is much more important than the value added to the acquiring company

40.   Business schools are high security prisons of the mind

41.   No matter how large and successful an organisation is, if it fails to adapt to change, then, like a dinosaur, it will become extinct

42. The size of a CEO's bonus is directly proportional to how much more the company would have lost had it not been for him or her

43. The less managers expect of their subordinates, the less they get

44. The amount of money spent to broadcast a television or radio commercial is inversely related to its truthfulness and relevance

45. All work and no play is a prescription for low quantity and quality of outputs

46. A bureaucrat is one who has the power to say 'no' but none to say 'yes'

47. Teleconferencing is an electronic way of wasting more time than is saved in travel

48. The more important the problem a manager asks consultants for help on, the less useful and more costly their solutions are likely to be

49. The distance between managers' offices is directly proportional to the difference between the ranks of their occupants

50. The *sine qua non* of leadership is talent, and talent cannot be taught

51. Managers who don't know how to measure what they want settle for wanting what they can measure

52. A great big happy family requires more loyalty than competence, but a great big happy business requires more competence than loyalty

53. If an organisation must grow, it is better for it to grow horizontally than vertically

54. Corporate development and corporate growth are not the same thing and neither requires the other

55. The uniqueness of an organisation lies more in what it hides than what it exposes

56. The telephone, which once facilitated communication, now increasingly obstructs it

57. Managers cannot learn from doing things right, only from doing things wrong

58. The principle objective of corporate executives is to provide themselves with the standard of living and quality of work life to which they aspire

59. The principal obstruction to an organisation getting to where its managers most want it to be lies in the minds of its managers

60. A corporation's external boundaries are generally much more penetrable than its internal ones

61. It is very difficult for those inside a box to think outside of it

62. The level of organisational development is directly proportional to the size of the gap between where the organisation is and where it wants to be

63. Most stated, corporate objectives are platitudes — they say nothing, but hide this fact behind words

64. Most corporations and business schools are less than the sum of their parts

65. Managers who try to make themselves look good by making others look bad, look worse than those they try to make look bad

66. The morality that many managers espouse in public is inversely proportional to the morality they practise in private

67. The higher their rank, the less managers perceive a need for continuing education, but the greater the need for it

68. The number of references and citations in a book is inversely proportional to the amount of thinking the author has done

69.   No computer is smarter than those who program it. Those who program computers are seldom smarter than those who try to use their output

70.   Managers cannot talk and listen at the same time; in fact, most managers find it very difficult to listen even when they are not talking

71.   Overheads, slides and PowerPoint projectors are *not* visual aids to managers. They transform managers into auditory aids to the visuals

72.   Conversations in a lavatory are more productive than those in the boardroom

73.   To managers an ounce of wisdom is worth a pound of understanding

74.   The press is the sword of Damocles that hangs over the head of every organisation

75.   The more managers try to get rid of what they don't want, the less likely they are to get what they do want

76.   Focusing on an organisation's 'core competency' diverts attention from its core competencies

77.   The greater the fee paid to corporate directors, the less their contributions are likely to be

78.   A manager's fear of computers is directly proportional to the square of his/her age

79.   Most managers know less about managing people than the conductor of an orchestra does

80.   Complex problems do not have simple solutions, only simple minded managers and their consultants think they do

81.   When nothing can make things worse, anything can make them better

The New Management f-Laws

82. To do more of what is not working currently, is to do more of what will not work in the future

In most cases when a strategy or tactic is failing it is blamed on a lack of resources. When more resources are allocated to it the result is usually to make its failure more expensive. An organisation arrives at maturity when it invests more in strategies and tactics that do not work than in ones that do. Witness public education in the United States.

Maturity is a state that most companies eventually reach. To break out of or avoid maturity, innovation is required: new products or services, new marketing or markets, more of what is different, not more of the same.

83. Those who successfully managed a company to maturity are unlikely to be able to manage it back to youth

The best that those who are managing a mature company can do is turn control over to those who have had no hand in bringing the company to its current state. Even a hysterical executive is more likely to succeed than a catatonic one.

It is not easy for an executive to admit to being an obstruction to further progress, particularly of a company whose previous growth he or she made possible. It would help if every company had a sainthood status that could be bestowed on those executives who have outlived their usefulness and hang on mercilessly.

84. Maldistribution of the quality of life at work reduces morale and results in poor quality products and services

Employees at all levels should be asked one simple question: 'Assuming you were guaranteed your current salary for the rest of your life no matter what you do, what would you do tomorrow?'

If the answer is anything but, 'I would come to work anyhow', their quality of life at work lacks something. When this question is asked of those at the top of an organisation, the answer is almost always: 'I would come to work anyhow'. When it is asked of those at the bottom, the answer is usually: 'I would get out of here like a bat out of hell'.

This leads to poor morale at lower levels in the organisation and amongst those who are making the goods and delivering the services to customers.

85. Greed at the top is the fuel used to increase the maldistribution of wealth within and between corporations, and within and between societies

The continued quest for income beyond what can be used to improve one's quality of life tends to reduce it.

One can accumulate more money than can be used to increase one's quality of life, but one can never accumulate too high a quality of life.

86. Viewing things differently is not a defect: it is an advantage

At any one time different managers will see the same thing in different ways; and the same manager will see different things in the same way at different times.

No two slices through an orange yield exactly the same view of its structure; but the more slices we examine, the more complete a picture of its structure we can formulate. It is through efforts to make different perceptions compatible that the whole truth can be approximated. The truth does not emerge from efforts to eliminate all perceptions but one. The truth is what makes it apparent that different perceptions of the same thing are, in fact, different perceptions of the same thing, not different things.

The head and tail of a coin are not views of different things, but different views of the same thing. Different views of the same problem lead to different ways of treating it, some better than others. It is only by viewing problems differently and evaluating those differences that the most effective treatments can be found.

87. It is better to dissolve a problem than solve it

There are four ways of treating a problem – absolution, resolution, solution, and dissolution – and the greatest of these is dissolution.

To **absolve** oneself of a problem is to ignore it and hope it will go away. This approach comes naturally to managers.

To **resolve** a problem is to do what was done last time a similar thing arose. It is an experience-based and common-sense approach. Problem resolution does not look for the best way of treating a problem, only one that is good enough.

To **solve** a problem involves a change in the behaviour of the organisation that has the problem, but leaves the nature of the organisation or its environment unchanged.

To **dissolve** a problem is to redesign the organisation that has the problem or its environment so the problem is eliminated and cannot reappear. An old Chinese proverb says that giving a hungry man a fish may solve his problem, but it will reoccur. Teaching him how to catch fish can dissolve his problem.

88. Giving managers the information needed to (dis)solve a problem does not necessarily improve their performance

We can only know what information is needed to (dis)solve a problem if we know how to (dis)solve it. If a way to (dis)solve a problem is known and the information required to do so is available, someone whose time is less valuable than a manager's can be given responsibility for (dis)solving it. For example, it can be given to a scientist, a staff member, a secretary or a computer.

Managers employ science but are not scientists. In other words, management is needed only where problems exists which we do not know how to (dis)solve.

89. The best way to find out how to get from here to there is to find out how to get from there to here

This counter-intuitive principle is apparent to children who quickly learn that the best way to solve a maze is to go from the exit to the entrance. It is equally true in corporate planning.

For example, how many tennis matches must be played in a tournament in which 64 players are entered? One can find the answer by working from the beginning to the end: there would be 32 first-round matches, 16 second round, 8 third round, 4 quarter finals, 2 semi-finals, and 1 final (making 63 matches in all).

Alternatively, we can work backwards from the end of the tournament; there must be 63 losers to obtain a winner, hence 63 matches.

90. The best place to begin an intellectual journey is at its end

And the best time to end it is when, working backwards, one reaches the beginning. The beginning is where one is now, of course.

Visionary managers always look ahead to a desired end. Whether they envision an entirely new product, a market that doesn't yet exist, or a more flexible organisation structure, they know where they want to be and then work backwards to find a way of getting there.

91. Necessity may be the mother of invention, but invention is the father of desire

People did not go around saying they wanted hand-held calculators, VCRs, digital watches, e-mail or mobile phones before they were invented. Their invention created the desire and alleged need for them.

We desire many things we do not need, and need many things we do not desire.

Needs are necessary for survival; desires are not, unless we desire what we need. We do not need most of the things we desire. We do not desire many of the things we need; we are not even conscious of needing them. Technology is driven more by desires than by needs.

92. Managers should never accept the output of a technologically-based support system unless they understand exactly what the system does and why

Many managers who are unwilling to accept advice or support from subordinates whose activities they do not fully understand, are nevertheless willing to accept support from computer-based systems of whose operations they are completely ignorant.

Management information systems are usually designed by technologists who understand neither management nor the difference between data and information. Combine such ignorance with a management that does not understand the system the technologists have designed, and one has a recipe for disaster or, if lucky, large expenditures that bring no return.

93. The amount of profit that can be got from the sale of a product or service is inversely proportional to the need for it

That's why luxury items provide the largest profit: for example, jewellery.

Marketing should try to make all the things we need desirable, and to make all the other things we desire but do not need, less destructive. This has a great deal more to do with ethics than technology.

Unfortunately, technology and ethics are the twain that seldom meet.

94. Meetings that share ignorance cannot produce knowledge

There is no amount of ignorance that, when aggregated, yields knowledge. Ten people who do not know how to do something are a much greater obstruction to learning how to do it than one. This is particularly true when they do not know that they do not know.

A manager who does not know and does not know that he/she does not know is a fool. One who does not know and thinks he/she does is a phony. A manager who knows but does not know that he/she knows is so rare that we have no name for it. Moreover, such a manager is usually unbearable.

Some managers see order when it is not there. Others do not see it when it is there. Those who see it when it is there usually have great difficulty in convincing others to this effect.

95. Employees, and even managers, are not expected to be smarter than their bosses

It usually takes great skill for people to disguise the fact that they are smarter than their bosses.

However, the ability to disguise the fact is a skill that is essential for survival in most organisations.

96. Continuous improvement is the longest distance between two points: where an organisation is and where it wants to be

Continuous improvement consists of a very large number of very small improvements. These can help maintain an organisation's leadership once it has achieved a leadership position, but not for long. Continuous improvement cannot make a leader out of a company that isn't one already. However, it can make followers out of organisations that adopt it.

Only large discontinuous improvements can elevate an organisation to leadership. These are creative acts, not imitative ones.

97. Benchmarking is a not-very-subtle form of imitation. It condemns organisations to following not leading

Imitation creates followers, not leaders. Imitation of a leader cannot close the gap because organisations that lead usually have a greater ability to improve themselves than do those that imitate them.

Taking the lead requires leaping over the other: a quantum leap. It requires not taking the time to do all the things that the leader has done, but taking the time to do something the leader has not done.

98. Consensus is practical, not necessarily principled, agreement

If consensus consisted of complete agreement between two or more decision-makers on the best possible decision, it would almost never be reached. Fortunately, consensus means agreeing that doing anything is better than doing nothing, or that doing nothing is better than doing anything. This makes it much easier to reach.

Conservatives generally believe that doing nothing is better than doing anything. Liberals generally believe that doing anything is better than doing nothing. Radicals believe that undoing everything and doing it over again is better than doing nothing or not doing anything.

Disagreements are often based on questions of fact. For example, does capital punishment decrease capital crimes? To reach consensus the agreement required is on the appropriateness of a proposed test to determine what the relevant facts are and an agreement to act as indicated by the facts.

99. In a classroom, the teacher learns most

We learn more on our own than by being taught. We learn our first language before going to school, without being taught it, but we do not learn a second language in school nearly as well. Being taught obstructs learning.

Anyone who has taught knows that the teacher learns the most in a classroom. Schools are upside down. Students should teach and faculty members should learn how to assist student learning.

Teachers should be motivating and facilitating the self-initiated learning of others. They should be a resource for students, used as the students see fit. But students should not be used by teachers as they see fit, especially when the students are mature managers. Learning how to use others as a resource is one of the most important things anyone, especially a manager, can learn.

Most important, we learn more out of, and after, school than in it, and more by doing than by listening. Most of what a manager uses at work is learned at work, not in business school; and it is learned with the help of others who have learned it at work.

100. There is never a better place to initiate a change than where the one who asks where the best place is, is

As the buck passes, it disintegrates, disappearing by the time it reaches its destination.

An organisation in which no one is willing to take responsibility for initiating change is paralysed, incapable of learning and adapting to change. It is in a catatonic stupor.

101. Risk aversion is a core competency of most managers

The pursuit of any significant change is never risk-free. But neither is the refusal to change, and this is the greater risk.

The prime principle for an individual's survival in most corporations is 'Cover thine arse'.

Professionals are generally willing, as a matter of principle, to try to change – even when facing disapproval, hence taking a personal risk. Non-professionals, as many managers are, as a matter of principle are generally not willing to face disapproval and personal risk.

102. The more managers believe in a democratic society the more they insist on autocratic corporations

Most managers in democratic societies insist that the society within which their organisations operate should operate openly and democratically. Nevertheless, they tend to manage their organisations secretively and autocratically.

The political structure of most corporations and not-for-profit organisations including schools, hospitals and government agencies remains hierarchical. And, even where organisations *have* become more heterarchical and their management more transparent, the behaviour of most managers or leaders under stress remains autocratic and secretive in nature.

Glasnost, like *Perestroika*, is as relevant to Western corporations as it was to the former Soviet Union.

103. The one thing that every individual and organisation must want is the ability to obtain whatever they want

To want anything is also to want the ability to obtain it: *competence*. Development is an increase in competence. Increases in competence require 4 types of progress:

1. **Science and technology**: the pursuit of the *truth* and the ability to use it efficiently in the pursuit of one's ends.

2. **Economics**: the pursuit of *plenty* and the resources to use the information, knowledge, and understanding that science and technology make available.

3. **Ethics and morality**: the pursuit of the *good*, peace on earth and peace of mind. These require the elimination of conflict so the pursuit of different ends provokes cooperation not conflict.

4. **Aesthetics**: the pursuit of *beauty and fun*, the stimulation and maintenance of the continuous pursuit of omni-competence.

Like a horse-drawn wagon, development cannot move faster than its slowest horse. In our society the slowest horse is aesthetics.

104. There is no such thing as risk-free agreement

Progress requires the exploration and exploitation of differences, including differences between colleagues and between subordinates and their bosses.

This, of course, always involves risk. There is no such thing as a risk-free disagreement with one's colleagues or boss.

What is less widely known is that there is no such thing as risk-free agreement. Executives who want clones as subordinates and subordinates who try to be clones of their bosses assure the preservation of the status quo. Groups, teams and meetings where dissent is discouraged or consensus is sought too quickly tend to end in 'groupthink' – an assumed consensus around a potentially bad decision.

Preserving the status quo and agreeing with bad decisions are both very risky ways to run a business these days.

105. CEOs should never select their successors

When superiors select successors they tend to select ones who are not likely to perform as well as they themselves did.

This may be done to assure retrospective admiration for that superior's superior performance (because executives like their reputations to be carried on the backs of their successors). Or it may be that the outgoing CEO cannot imagine that a very different approach could work as well as – or better than – their own (so they will not appoint someone who takes that different approach).

Either way, selecting our successors is as dangerous as selecting our children.

106. To managers, an ounce of information is worth a pound of data

Data are symbols that represent the properties of objects and events. They are to information what iron ore is to iron: nothing can be done with data until they are processed into information.

Information also consists of symbols that represent the properties of objects and events, but these are symbols that have been processed into a potentially useful message. Information is contained in descriptions; answers to questions that begin with such words as *who*, *where*, *when*, *what*, and *how many*.

Most relevant information can be condensed significantly without loss of content. Irrelevant information can be condensed to zero without loss of content. Therefore, filtration and condensation are the two most important processes that can be applied to information. These, however, are considered to be irrelevant by those who provide managers with information. For them value and volume are synonymous.

107. To managers, an ounce of knowledge is worth a pound of information

Knowledge is contained in instructions, answers to *how to* questions. To know that a car won't run is information; to know how to make it work when it doesn't is knowledge.

But knowledge presupposes information just as information presupposes data. Without the information that a car needs fixing, relevant knowledge would not be applied to it. The function of knowledge is to enable one to make efficient choices between alternatives revealed by information. Knowledge also provides criteria for determining the relevance of information; it identifies the information required to use what is known. So information and knowledge, like Punch and Judy, presuppose each other, have no practical value when separated from each other except on quiz shows and examinations given in schools.

What an individual knows becomes organisational knowledge only when it is accessible to anybody else in the organisation who has a need for it, even if the source of that knowledge is no longer part of the organisation.

108. To managers, an ounce of understanding is worth a pound of knowledge

Understanding is contained in explanations, answers to *why* questions. To know how a car works is knowledge; to know why it was designed to work the way it does is understanding.

Knowledge of how a thing works requires knowing its structure, how its parts interact. Understanding the nature of a thing means knowing its functions in the larger systems it is part of. For example, a car's function could be: to enable people to go from one place to another on land under their control and in privacy. It is part of a transportation system. The function of the accelerator is to serve the function of the car, hence the purpose of the driver. Knowledge lets us make things work; understanding lets us make things work the way we want them to.

The function of a corporation is to create and distribute wealth in the society it operates in and to promote the development of its stakeholders and that society. Productive employment is the only way known to man of simultaneously producing and distributing wealth. All other ways of distributing wealth consume it.

109. To managers an ounce of wisdom is worth a pound of understanding

This makes an ounce of wisdom worth 65,536 ounces of data, using the previous three f-Laws. Wisdom is contained in value statements, e.g. aphorisms and proverbs. It lets us perceive and evaluate the long-term as well as short-term consequences of what we do. It induces us to want to pursue things of lasting value. It enables us to make short-run sacrifices for long-run gains. It prevents our sacrificing the future for the present.

Knowledge enables us to make things work; understanding enables us to make things work the way we want; wisdom enables us to want the 'right' things, things that increase our ability to obtain what we and others need and want.

Information, knowledge and understanding enable us to do things right, to be efficient, but wisdom enables us to do the right things, to be effective. Science pursues data, information, knowledge and understanding: what is truth; but the humanities pursue wisdom: what is right.

110. Giving managers the information they want may not improve their performance

The genius of managers, where it exists, lies in their ability to manage efficiently systems they do not completely know or understand. Where knowledge and understanding are lacking, there is no criterion for determining what constitutes relevant information. Without criteria it is intuition that plays the key role. The quality of their intuitions differentiates managers more than the quality of what they know and understand.

When managers who lack relevant knowledge and understanding are asked what information they want, they say, 'Everything'. The result is an increase in information overload and in the time that must be spent filtering out what is relevant.

The genius of science lies in its ability to manage systems that are understood. But science is incapable of managing efficiently any system that is not understood. So, science gives management the platform from which, using intuition, it can jump into uncertainty. But it should be remembered that managers jump, not scientists, and so the risks and responsibilities associated with decision-making are not shared equally. In fact, they are not shared at all.

111. Rightsizing treats a symptom but not the disease

Rightsizing is a euphemism for downsizing, which is itself a euphemism. To rightsize is to reduce over-employment, which is a symptom, not a disease. The disease consists of the presence of internal units that are monopolistic providers of essential services to other internal units that do not pay for these services directly.

Internal service monopolies are subsidised by an amount proportional to their size. So they try to grow continually by creating 'make work'. Because users have no choice of supplier, the suppliers are not responsive to their users' needs and desires.

Furthermore, they have little incentive to serve them efficiently. Downsizing may reduce the size of internal service units but it does not change their *modus operandi* – which involves generating make-work and adding excess personnel. When competition forces corporations to cut costs, they often resort to downsizing because their internal monopolies resort to upsizing. Downsizing is endemic to organisations whose internal service providers are bureaucratic monopolies. An internal market economy is the only effective way of eliminating bureaucratic monopolies.

112. Improving communication between the parts of an organisation may destroy it

The more information hostile parties have about one another, the more harm each can inflict on the other. If in war neither party had any information about the other they would be unable to inflict any harm or destruction on the other. Of course, it is equally true that the more information friendly parties have about each other the more help they can give each other. Therefore, communication has value only among cooperating parties.

However, as Peter Drucker once observed, there is more conflict within corporations than between them, and it is generally less ethical. Therefore, unless such conflict is eliminated, improved communication within a firm can hurt it, even destroy it.

Effective alignment of objectives is essential if communication is to benefit communicating parties. Such alignment can only occur when performance of the whole organisation is the primary criterion employed in evaluating performance of any of the parts.

113. The stability of a family business and of the family that owns it are inversely proportional to the number of family members employed in the business

Sons seldom believe that father knows best or, as a matter of fact, that anyone other than themselves does. A family business brings out the worst in relatives, particularly in those whose best is not very good. The competition for power in the business among siblings tends to carry over into the family and is as destructive to the family as it is to the business.

Members of a family know each other's weaknesses better than the weaknesses of any outsider. Therefore, they tend to trust each other less than outsiders, and with good reason.

Competence is not an inherited characteristic. It tends to diminish with successive generations. A competent offspring is a mutant, not a product of systemic evolution.

114. Communication is never good in itself

This is a common misapprehension.

Communication is only a means to ends that may be bad as well as good. It should be kept in mind that although some communication may be good, there is an amount of it, as for anything, that is bad.

Witness spam!

115. The prominence of a business author is proportional to the number of times he or she has published the same article or book

Nothing breeds more business books than a successful business book. Follow-ups are like sequels to a successful movie. They continue as long as the author/producer is alive and those who read/saw the first book/movie no longer remember it.

A change in punctuation or format is sufficient reason for a new edition of a successful book no matter how bad it is. But no change is sufficient reason for republishing an unsuccessful book, no matter how good it is.

This last statement is not quite true: if more sex could be introduced into unsuccessful books they just might sell – especially if illustrated. But it is as hard to make books on management sexy as it is to make managers sexy.

Oh, and by the way, no author has ever read all the books he or she cites.

116. Organisations fail more often because of what they have not done than because of what they have done

Similarly, it is worse to deny a truth than accept a falsehood. But errors of omission are seldom recorded and accounted for. So, executives who cannot get away unpunished for doing something they should not have done, can usually get away with not doing something they should have done.

Since errors of commission are the only type of mistake accounted for, a security-seeking manager's optimal strategy is to avoid such errors by doing as little as possible, including nothing. The most successful executives are those who can create the appearance of doing a great deal without doing anything. Herein lies the root of an organisation's disinclination to change.

117. The quality of a business school is inversely proportional to the average amount of teaching its faculty does

The higher the ranking of a business school, the lower is the average teaching load of its faculty members and the less time they spend at the institution. The moral is clear: business schools would attain the highest possible rank if no teaching was done and faculty members were never present.

It is ironic that schools that try to minimise the amount of teaching their faculty must do, also try to maximise the amount of teaching to which their students are subjected. This maximises the number of faculty members required per square student. Business schools give students the illusion of relevant learning: an illusion later dispelled at work. Business school students learn a vocabulary that enables them to speak authoritatively on subjects they do not understand. They also learn a set of principles that have demonstrated their ability to withstand large amounts of disconfirming evidence. Finally, business schools provide a ticket of admission to a job on which relevant learning can begin.

118. Successful management consultants are ones who support managers' unsupportable beliefs

Managers' strongest opinions are ones for which there is no supporting evidence. This follows from the fact that the reputations of managers depend to a large extent on their ability to convey the impression of infallibility to their peers and superiors. (Their subordinates *always* know how fallible they are.)

Managers' infallibility-complex is reflected in the fact that they never express doubt or consult a reference or authority when confronted with a problem while in the presence of others.

All this explains why managers prefer consultants who produce the appearance of proof for what those same managers accept without proof.

119. Problems are not objects of experience, but mental constructs extracted from it by analysis

Problems are abstractions. What managers actually experience are messes, which are complex systems of interacting problems. Problems are to messes what atoms are to desks. We experience desks, not the atoms they are made of; we experience messes, not the problems they are made of.

No problem can be solved without affecting others in the system of which it is a part, usually without exacerbating them. A solution to a problem taken separately can create a much more serious problem than the problem solved.

One can get rid of a bad heart by having it removed. One can avoid food poisoning by not eating. Solving problems taken separately can be a very dangerous thing.

120. It is better to control the future imperfectly than to forecast it perfectly

For example, we would rather work in a building in which the weather is controlled, than out of doors even if we had a perfect forecast of the weather and access to all the clothing we would want.

Control of oneself and one's immediate environment eliminates the need to forecast or control the less immediate environment. And, indeed, the rapidity of change makes reliable forecasting harder than ever to do well.

The objective of planning should not be to prepare for a future that is out of our control, but to control that future in the way that buildings control future weather.

121. Competition is conflict embedded in cooperation; the more conflict there is, the more cooperation there is

Two tennis players in a friendly match are in conflict with respect to winning. But they cooperate over a more important shared objective: recreation and exercise. The more intense their conflict, the more fun and exercise they derive from the match. If the cooperative objectives, fun and exercise, do not dominate the conflicting objective, winning, then the match becomes a fight.

Competition is conflict according to rules designed to ensure cooperation. When the rules are broken, cooperation evaporates and conflict remains. Competition needs a referee to ensure the rules are followed. In economic competition conflict between suppliers is intended to serve the interests of consumers. If competitors collude to bilk consumers, as in price fixing, they stop competing, cooperate with each other and conflict with consumers. Government is the referee that makes the rules to prevent economic competition turning into conflict or pure cooperation. But government is a supplier of regulations for sale in the lobby.

122. How far an organisation can evade government regulations is proportional to the amount it contributed to the election of successful candidates

This f-law has a number of corollaries:

Lobbyists are lawyers who no longer practice law; they buy it. Elected officials whose campaigns are financed by corporations sell the law to them. Together they form a vicious circle from which the public cannot escape. The circumference of the circle is directly proportional to the number of organisations the officials are willing to 'accommodate'.

Executives who engage in evasions of the law sometimes 'get caught'. This usually involves a length of time between their exposure and trial that exceeds their time to retirement or death.

Those executives who serve a term in prison wear it like a badge of honour when they come out. They are taken to be martyrs to the corporate cause.

123. In advertising, all competing products or services have a common property: each is better than the others

It follows that every product or service on the market is also worse than all the others. Comparative ads are intended to support a product's claim for superiority over the one generally recognised as the best in the class. All this does is firmly establish the one considered to be the best in its class as the best in its class.

Each advertiser emphasises the positive and ignores the negative. There is no product/service that is not better than its competition relative to some property. This property is broadcast. What is suppressed are all the properties with respect to which the product or service is worse than its competition.

The life of a product or service is reduced by claims which are not substantiated by its use, or which are irrelevant. For example, it was claimed of the first ball-point pen on the market that it could be used to make nine carbon copies and could even write under water. What it did do well was leak. Like the shirts that held it, the pen had a very short life.

Appendix: Additional Reading

Other recommended books by Russ Ackoff:

Management f-Laws ~ 2007 (a collection of 80 laws in the same vein as those you've read here)

Ackoff's f-Laws: The Cake ~ Russell Ackoff
Redesigning Society ~ 2003
Re-Creating the Corporation ~ 1999
The Democratic Corporation ~ 1994
The Art of Problem Solving ~ 1978

Other books on Systems Thinking and organisations:

Delivering Public Services that Work Vol I (Systems Thinking in the Public Sector: Case Studies) ~ Peter Middleton (ed), 2010

Growing Wings on the Way: Systems Thinking for Messy Situations ~ Rosalind Armson, 2011

The Search for Leadership ~ William Tate, 2009

Systems Thinking in the Public Sector ~ John Seddon, 2008

Systems Thinking: Creative Holism for Managers ~ M.C. Jackson, 2003

The Fifth Discipline ~ Peter Senge, 1999

Systems Thinking – Managing Chaos and Complexity: a Platform for Designing Business Architecture ~ Jamshid Gharajedaghi, 1999

Broader reading on Systems Thinking:

General System Theory: Foundations, Development, Applications ~ Ludwig Von Bertalanffy, 1976

Small Arcs of Larger Circles ~ Nora Bateson, 2016

Systems Thinking, Systems Practice ~ Peter Checkland, 1981

The Web of Life ~ Fritjof Capra, 1997

Related thinking about organisations:

Complexity theory:

Complexity, Organizations and Change ~ Elizabeth McMillan, 2004
Complexity and Creativity in Organizations ~ Ralph Stacey, 1996
Adventures in Complexity ~ Lesley Kuhn, 2009

Chaos theory:

The Essence of Chaos ~ Edward Lorenz, 1996
Chaos Theory in the Social Sciences ~ L. Douglas Kiel and Euel W. Elliott, 1997

Design thinking:

Design Thinking ~ Red Hat Magazine, 2006
The Innovation Acid Test ~ Andrew Jones, 2008

Cultural theory:

Organising and Disorganising ~ Michael Thompson, 2008
How Institutions Think ~ Mary Douglas, 1986

Triarchy theory:
The Three Ways of Getting Things Done: Hierarchy, Heterarchy and Responsible Autonomy in Organizations ~ Gerard Fairtlough, 2007

Systems Thinking websites:

www.systemsthinking.co.uk
www.thinking.net/Systems_Thinking/systems_thinking.html
www.thesystemsthinkingreview.co.uk
www.systems-thinking.org/intst/int.htm
www.systems-thinking.de
www.triarchypress.net

About Triarchy Press

Triarchy Press is an independent publisher of alternative thinking about government, organisations and society. Other titles include:

Management f-Laws ~ Russell Ackoff, Herb Addison, Sally Bibb
Ackoff's f-Laws: The Cake ~ Russell Ackoff
Differences That Make a Difference ~ Russell Ackoff
Systems Thinking in the Public Sector ~ John Seddon
Delivering Public Services that Work ~ Peter Middleton
The Search for Leadership ~ William Tate
The Decision Loom ~ Vince Barabba
The Organisational Leadership Toolkit ~ William Tate
Adventures in Complexity ~ Lesley Kuhn
Organising and Disorganising ~ Michael Thompson
Small Arcs of Larger Circles ~ Nora Bateson
Strategic Foresight ~ Patricia Lustig
The Whitehall Effect ~ John Seddon

www.triarchypress.net

Milton Keynes UK
Ingram Content Group UK Ltd.
UKHW021935300424
441979UK00010B/176

9 780956 263155